Alexander Crummell

The Relations and Duties of Free Colored Men in America to Africa

A letter to Charles B. Dunbar

Alexander Crummell

The Relations and Duties of Free Colored Men in America to Africa
A letter to Charles B. Dunbar

ISBN/EAN: 9783744751926

Printed in Europe, USA, Canada, Australia, Japan

Cover: Foto ©ninafisch / pixelio.de

More available books at **www.hansebooks.com**

THE
RELATIONS AND DUTIES

OF

FREE COLORED MEN IN AMERICA
TO AFRICA.

———•—•—•———

A LETTER

TO

CHARLES B. DUNBAR, M. D., ESQ.,

OF NEW YORK CITY.

BY

THE REV. ALEX. CRUMMELL, B. A.

"Quo res cunque cadent, unum et commune periculum
Una salus ambobus erit."—VIRGIL.

HARTFORD:
PRESS OF CASE, LOCKWOOD AND COMPANY.
1861.

NOTE.

REV. MR. CRUMMELL, the author of the following pages, is a pure African—educated by private charity at Queens' College, England—where he became acquainted with President Roberts and others, from whom he obtained such information of Liberia as determined him to make that country his permanent residence. Before he received his University education, he was for a time the pastor of a Protestant Episcopal congregation of colored people in New York, and is well known to the colored people of that city, and to many in other parts of the country.

" It is in Africa that this evil must be rooted out—by African hands and African exertions chiefly that it can be destroyed."

McQUEEN.—" View of Northern Central Africa."

" We may live to behold the nations of Africa engaged in the calm occupations of industry, and in the pursuit of a just and legitimate commerce; we may behold the beams of science and philosophy breaking in upon their land, which at some happier period, in still later times, may blaze with full lustre, and joining their influence to that of PURE RELIGION, may illuminate and invigorate the most distant extremities of that immense continent."—WM. PITT.

LETTER.

HIGH SCHOOL, MT. VAUGHAN, CAPE PALMAS, ⎱
LIBERIA, 1st Sept., 1860.   ⎰

MY DEAR SIR,—It is now many months since I received a letter from you, just as you was about sailing from our shores for your home. In that note you requested me to address you a letter setting forth my views concerning Liberia, suggesting at the same time that such a letter might prove interesting to many of our old friends and school-mates in New York. I have not forgotten your request, although I have not·heretofore complied with it. Though convinced of the need and possible usefulness of such a letter as you asked from me, I have shrunk from a compliance with your request. Not to mention other grounds of reluctance, let me say here that I have felt it a venturesome thing to address four hundred thousand men ; albeit, it be indirectly through you. Neither my name, position, nor any personal qualities, give me authority thus to do. The only excuse I have is the depth and solemnity of all questions connected with Africa. I see that no one else of our race has done it ; perhaps I may be pardoned for assuming so great a task.

I may add here that I address the " Free Colored Men of America," because I am identified with them ; and not because I feel that *they*, especially, and above all the other sons of Africa, in distant lands, are called upon for zeal and interest in her behalf. It is the exaggeration of the relation of *American* black men to Africa, which has turned the hearts of many of her own children from her. Your duties, in this respect are no greater than those of our West Indian, Haytian, and eventually our Brazilian brethren. Whatever in this letter applies to our brethren in the United States, applies in an equal degree to them. But I am not the man to address them. I fear I *presume*, even in writing this letter to American black men, and have only just now concluded to do so by the encouragement I have received in two pleasant interviews with Mr. Campbell and Dr. Delany.

And even now it is with doubt and diffidence that I conclude to send you this communication. My reluctancy has arisen chiefly from a consideration of the claim put forth by leading colored men in the United States, to the effect "that it is unjust to disturb their residence in the land of their birth, by a continual call to go to Africa." This claim is, in my opinion, a most just one. Three centuries residence in a country seems clearly to give any people a right to their nationality therein, without disturbance. Our brethren in America have other claims besides this; they have made large contributions to the clearing of their country; they have contributed by sweat and toil to the wealth thereof; and by their prowess and their blood, they have participated in the achievement of its liberties. But their master right lies in the fact that they are Christians; and one will have to find some new page and appendage to the Bible, to get the warrant for Christians to repel and expatriate Christians, on account of blood, or race, or color. In fact, it seems to me a most serious thing to wantonly trench upon rights, thus solemnly and providentially guaranteed a people, that is, by a constant, ceaseless, fretting iteration of a repelling sentiment.

Of course I do not intend anything akin to this in my letter. I need not insult the intellect and conscience of any colored man who thinks it his duty to labor for his race on American soil, by telling him that it is his duty to come to Africa. If he is educated up to the ideas of responsibility and obligation, he knows his duty better than I do. And, indeed, generally, it is best to leave individuals to themselves as to the *details* of obligation and responsibility.

" The primal duties shine aloft like stars ; " and it is only when men *will* not see them, we are bound to repeat and re-utter them, until the souls of men are aroused, and they are moved to moral resolution and to noble actions. But as to the *mode, form* and *manner* of meeting their duties, let the common sense of every man decide it for himself.

My object in writing this letter is not to vex any of our brethren by the iteration of the falsehood that America is not their home ; nor by the misty theory, "that they will all yet have to come to Liberia." I do not even intend to invite any one to Liberia ; glad as I would be to see around me many of the wise and sterling men I know in the U. States, who would be real acquisitions to this nation, and as much as I covet their society. I am not putting in a plea for Colonization. My object is quite different ; in fact it is not a strict compliance with the terms of your letter, for I shall have but little to say about Liberia. But believing that *all* men hold some relation to the land of their Fathers, I wish to call the attention of the sons of Africa in America to their "RELATIONS AND DUTY TO THE LAND OF THEIR FATHERS."

And even on such a theme I know I must prepare myself for the rebuff from many—"Why talk to *us* of Fatherland ? What have we to do with Africa ? We are not Africans; we are Americans. You ask no peculiar interest on the part of Germans, Englishmen, the Scotch, the Irish, the Dutch, in the land of their fathers ; why then do you ask it of us ? "

Alas for us, as a race ! so deeply harmed have we been by oppression, that we have lost the force of strong, native prin-ciples, and prime natural affections. Because exaggerated contempt has been poured upon us, we too become apt pupils in the school of scorn and contumely. Because repudiation of the black man has been for centuries the wont of civilized nations, black men themselves get shame at their origin and shrink from the terms which indicate it.

Sad as this is, it is not to be wondered at. "Oppression " not only "makes a wise man mad," it robs him also of his self-respect. And this is our loss ; but having emerged from slavery, it is our duty to cast off its grave-clothes and resist its deadly influences.

Our ancestors were unfortunate, miserable and benighted; but nothing more. Their history was a history, not of ignominy and disgrace, but of heathenism and benightedness. And even in that state they exhibited a nobleness of native character, they cherished such virtues, and manifested so much manliness and bravery, that the civilized world is now magnanimous enough to recognize such traits; and its greatest men are free to render their warm eulogies.*

When these colored men question the duty of interest in Africa because they are not Africans, I beg to remind them of the kindred duty of self-respect. And my reply to such queries as I have mentioned above is this: 1. That there is no need of asking the interest of Englishmen, Germans, Dutchmen and others in the land of their Fathers; because they have this interest, and are always proud to cherish it. And 2nd, I remark that the abject state of Africa is a most real and touching appeal to *any* heart for sympathy and aid. It is an appeal, however, which comes with a double force to every civilized man who has negro blood flowing in his veins.

Africa lies low and is wretched. She is the maimed and crippled arm of humanity. Her great powers are wasted. Dislocation and anguish have reached every joint. Her condition in every point calls for succor; moral, social, domestic, political, commercial, intellectual. Whence shall flow aid, mercy, advantage to her? Here arises the call of duty and obligation to colored men. Other people may, if they choose, forget the homes of their sires; for almost every European nation is now reaping the fruits of a thousand years civilization. Every one of them can spare thousands and even millions of their sons to build up civilization in Australia, Canada, New Zealand, South Africa, or Victoria. But Africa is the victim of her heterogenous idolatries. Africa is wasting away beneath the accretions of civil and moral miseries. Darkness covers the land and gross darkness the people. Great social evils uni-

---

* For a most able and discriminating article upon this topic, see " WESTMINSTER REVIEW," January 7, 1842, Art., Dr. Arnold. Also, those humane and truthful Essays of Mr. HEAPS.—" FRIENDS IN COUNCIL, vol. 2.

versally prevail. Confidence and security are destroyed. Licentiousness abounds everywhere. Molock rules and reigns throughout the whole Continent; and by the ordeal of Sassywood, Fetiches, human sacrifices and devil-worship is devouring men, women and little children. They have not the Gospel. They are living without God. The cross has never met their gaze ; and its consolations have never entered their hearts, nor its everlasting truths cheered their deaths.

And all this only epitomizes the miseries of Africa, for it would take a volume to detail and enumerate them. But this is sufficient to convince any son of Africa that the land of our fathers is in great spiritual need, and that those of her sons who haply have ability to aid in her restoration, will show mercy to her, and perform an act of filial love and tenderness which is but their " reasonable service."

I have two objects in view in addressing you this letter : *one* relates to the temporal, material interests of adventurous, enterprising, colored men ; and the *other* pertains to the best and most abiding interests of the million masses of heathen on this continent—I mean their evangelization.

First, I am to speak with reference to the temporal, and material interests of adventurous, enterprising and aspiring men in the United States of America. I wish to bring before such persons reasons why they should feel interest in Africa. These reasons are not, I am free to confess, directly and distinctively philanthropic ; although I do, indeed, aim at human well-being through their force and influence. But I appeal now more especially to the hopes, desires, ambition, and aspirations of such men. I am referring to that sentiment of self-regard which prompts to noble exertions for support and superiority. I am aiming at that principle of SELF LOVE which spurs men on to self advantage and self aggrandizement; a principle which, in its normal state and in its due degree, to use the words of BUTLER, " is as just and morally good as any affection whatever." In fine, I address myself to all that class of sentiments in the human heart which creates a thirst for wealth, position, honor, and power. I desire the auxiliary aid of this class of persons, and this class of motives, for it is such influences and agencies which are calculated to advance the material growth of Africa. She needs skill, enterprise, energy, *worldly* talent, to raise her; and these applied here to her needs and circumstances, will prove the handmaid of Religion, and will serve the great purposes of civilization and enlightenment through all her borders.

There seems to me to be a natural call upon the children of Africa in foreign lands, to come and participate in the opening treasures of the land of their fathers. Though these treasures are the manifest gift of God to the negro race, yet that race reaps but the most partial measure of their good and advantage. It has always been thus in the past, and now as the resources of Africa are being more and more developed, the extent of *our* interest therein is becoming more and more diminutive. The slave-trade is interdicted throughout Christendom; the chief powers of earth have put a lien upon the system of slavery; interest and research in Africa have reached a state of intensity; mystery has been banished from some of her most secret quarters; sunlight, after ages of darkness, has burst in upon the charmed regions of her wealth and value; and yet the negro, on his native soil, is but " a hewer of wood and drawer of water;" and the sons of Africa in foreign lands, inane and blinded, suffer the adventurous foreigner, with greed and glut, to jostle him aside, and to seize, with skill and effect, upon their own rightful inheritance.

For three centuries and upwards, the civilized nations of the earth have been engaged in African commerce. Traffic on the coast of Africa anticipated the discoveries of Columbus. From Africa the purest gold got its characteristic three hundred years ago. From Africa dyes of the greatest value have been carried to the great manufacturing marts of the world. From Africa palm oil is exported by thousands of tons; and now as the observant eye of commerce is becoming more and more fastened upon this continent, grain, gums, oils of divers kinds, valuable woods, copper and other ore, are being borne from the soil to meet the clamorous demands of distant marts.

The chief item of commerce in this continent has been the " slave trade." The coast of Africa has been more noted for this than for anything else. Ever since 1600, the civilized nations of the earth have been transporting in deadly holds, in poisonous and pestilential cabins, in "perfidious barks," millions of our race to foreign lands. This trade is now almost universally regarded as criminal; but in the light of commercial prudence and pecuniary advantage, the slave trade was as great a piece of folly as it was a crime; for almost beneath their eyes, yea, doubtless, often immediately in their sight, were lying treasures, rivaling far the market value of the flesh and blood they had been so eager to crowd beneath their hatches.

Africa is as rich in resources as India is; not as yet as valuable in products, because she is more unenlightened, and has a less skilful population. But so far as it respects mineral and vegetable capacity, there seems to me but little, if any doubt that Africa more than rivals the most productive lands on the globe.

Let me set before you, though briefly, some of the valuable articles of West African trade. I must remind you, however, of three things; *first*, that the soil, the rocks, and the flora of Africa have not had the advantage of scientific scrutiny, and as a consequence but little is known as yet of her real worth and wealth in these respects. *Second*, that West African trade is only in a nascent state—that it comes from but a slight fringe of the coast, while the rich interior yields, as yet, but a reluctant hold upon the vast and various treasures it possesses. And *third*, that such is the mysterious secrecy American and English houses retain and *enjoin* upon this subject, that even approximation to the facts of the case is remote and distant.

The following Table is an attempt to classify valuable products and articles of present trade. Nearly every article mentioned has come under my own personal inspection; the exceptions are not over a dozen and a half.

Nuts.	Dyes and Dyewood.	Gums and Wax.	Animals.
Palm Nut.	Camwood.	Beeswax.	Oxen.
Ground Nut.	Barwood.	Grove Tree.	Sheep.
Cocoa Nut.	Indigo.	India Rubber.	Hogs.
Cold Nut. .	Christmas nut.	Gutta Percha.	Goats.
Castor Nut.	And divers oth-	Copal.	Fowls.
	er colors, blue,	Mastic.	Ducks.
	red, yellow, &	Senegal.	Pigeons.
	brown.		

Skins.	Grains.	Fruits.	Vegetables.
Bullock.	Rice.	Oranges.	Yams.
Sheep.	Maize.	Lemons.	Cassada.
Deer.	Millet.	Plantains.	Potatoes.
Monkey.		Bananas.	Tan yah.
Leopard.		Citrons.	
Gazelle.		Limes.	
Squirrel.		Guavas.	
Raccoon.		Pine Apples.	
Lion.		Papaw.	
		Mango Plums.	
		Alligator Pear.	
		Bread Nut.	
		Tamarind.	

Timber.	Minerals.	Special articles connected with trade & domestic use.	Fish.
Teak.	Iron.	Sugar Cane.	Mackerel.
Ebony.	Copper.	Coffee.	Mango Perch.
Lignum Vitæ.	Gold.	Cocoa.	Caualla.
Mahogany.		Pepper.	Gripper.
Brimstone.		Cotton.	Herring.
Rosewood.		Tobacco.	Mullet.
Walnut.			Chub.
Hickory.			Perch.
Oak.			Pike.
Cedar.			Trout.
Unevah.			Cod.
Mangrove.			Skate.
			Eels.
			Oysters.

I can not dismiss these Tables without a few remarks relative to some few prominent items they enumerate; I mean the Palm Nut and Oil, Cotton, Indian Corn, and Sugar Cane.

Palm Oil.—This article, more than any other West African product, shows the rapidity with which legitimate commerce has sprung up on the coast of Africa. A few years ago palm oil was an insignificant item in the coast trade.* Now it is an article which commands whole fleets of sailing vessels, seeks the auxiliary aid of steamers, and effects most powerfully the commerce of England, France, and the United States.

I copy several items pertaining to this export from a report of a former acquaintance and correspondent, the late Mr. Consul Campbell, of Lagos. The report, as will be seen, includes several other items besides palm oil, and it refers exclusively to Lagos.

SHIPPED FROM LAGOS DURING 1857.

			Value.
13,097	casks of Palm Oil,	4,942 tons,	£222,390
1,053	Elephant Tusks,	24,118 lbs.,	4,220
868	bales of Cotton,	114,848 lbs.,	3,490
			230,200
50,000	native Cotton Cloths,		25,000
	Total value of exports from Lagos,		£255,200

Palm Oil—

From the Benin River,	2,650	tons,
" Palma,	3,250	"
" Badagry,	1,250	"
" Porto Novo, Appi, Vista, &c.,	4,500	"
" Whydah,	2,500	"
" Ahguay and neighbor'g ports,	2,500	"
	16,650 tons,	£732,600

150,000 country Cloths of native manu-
facture from above ports,   75,000

                                                      £1,062,800

* In 1808, the quantity imported into England was only 200 (two hundred) tons.

Of the above productions there was shipped from Lagos in the year—

	1856.	1857.	Increase.
Palm Oil,	3,884 tons.	4,942 tons.	1,058 tons.
Ivory,	16,057 lbs.	24,118 lbs.	8,061 lbs.
Cotton,	34,491 lbs.	114,844 lbs.	81,353 lbs.

Palm Oil from other ports—

	1856.	1857.	Increase.
Benin River,	2,500 tons.	2,650 tons.	150 tons.
Palma,	2,250 "	3,250 "	1,000 "
Badagry,	1,250 "	·1,250 "	
Porto Novo, &c.,	4,000 "	4,500 "	500 "
Whydah,	2,500 "	2,500 "	
Ahguay, &c.,	1,800 "	2,500 "	700 "
	14,300 tons.	16,650 tons.	2,350 tons.
From Lagos,	3,884 "	4,942 "	1,058 "

Total shipment in 1857,   21,592 tons.   3,408 tons.

The export of Oil and Nuts from SIERRA LEONE, is as follows:

PALM OIL EXPORTED FROM SIERRA LEONE DURING THE YEARS.

1850,	285,032	gallons,
1851,	212,577	"
1852,	307,988	"
1853,	181,438	"
1854,	304,406	"
1855,	364,414	"
1856,	463,140	"

Total,   2,118,985 gallons, equal to 6,835 tons.

Custom House, Sierra Leone, 18th February, 1857.

PORT OF FREETOWN, SIERRA LEONE.

QUANTITY OF PALM-NUT KERNELS EXPORTED FROM THE COLONY, AS FOLLOWS, VIZ.:

1850,	4,096	bushels,
1851,	2,925	"
1852,	46,727	"

1853,	29,699	bushels.
1854,	25,399½	"
1855,	65,388	"
1856,	90,282	"

Total,   264,516½ bushels, equal to 6,612 tons.
Customs, Sierra Leone, 30th January, 1857.

I have no reliable information of the amount of oil exported at the present; but I do not think I shall be far from the point of accuracy, if I put it down at 60,000 tons, which, at the probable value of £45 per ton, equals £2,700,000.

COTTON.—Next to palm oil, cotton is now commanding more attention than any other article. The interesting fact with regard to this staple is that it excites as much interest in Africa as it does in England and America. There are few things in the history of trade more important, more interesting, morally as well as commercially, than the impetus which has recently been given to the growth of cotton.

In 185–, Mr. Consul Campbell made a statement of the probable amount of cotton exported from West Africa. I have to rely upon my memory for the items of that statement; and, if I mistake not, he stated that the people of Abbeokuta exported nigh 200,000 country cloths annually. These cloths are purchased for transportation to Brazil, where there are thousands of African slaves who still dress in the same style as when at their homes. He supposed that full 200,000 country cloths were manufactured for *home* use, which would make the probable number manufactured in Africa, 400,000. And he calculated 2½ lbs. as the average weight of each country cloth;—and 400,000 × 2½ = 1,000,000 lbs. of cotton *manufactured* by the natives of interior Africa, in *one* locality, that is Yoruba. Doubtless as much more is allowed to grow and run to waste, unused.

Now these facts, to a partial extent, were well known in Liberia, for our merchants are accustomed to purchasing " country cloths," as they are called, and selling them to foreign traders; but Consul Campbell's statements far exceed any realities we have ever thought of, and show that interior

Africa is as great a field for the production of cotton, as America or India.

SUGAR CANE.—To what extent West Africa is to become a sugar-producing country it is difficult to conjecture. Many, doubtless, have grave doubts whether this will ever be the case; for my own part I have no misgivings upon the point, that is, its capability of becoming a great sugar-producing country. The natives grow it in all the country about Cape Palmas, and frequently bring cane to the American settlements for sale. With some small encouragement, and a little stimulus, it could easily be made a staple here. My opinions have been strengthened by some observations made in a recent missionary tour. I found cane but little inferior to that grown on the St. Paul's river, growing in nearly all the towns and villages through which I passed, forty, fifty, and sixty miles in the interior. On inquiry, I learned that it is grown by the natives in the interior, two hundred miles back. Dr. Livingstone, in his journal, states a like fact concerning the natives in South Africa.*

What a germ have we here for systematic labor, plodding industry, the proper direction of the acquisition principle, and thereby, of civilization and christianity, if only a company of right-minded men were settled on the Cavalla, prepared for the production of sugar, willing to stimulate national energy, and at the same time to uplift and enlighten the heathen!

MAIZE.—What is the case respecting sugar cane equally pertains to corn. It is grown plenteously and extensively in West Africa. On the Cavalla river it is planted with rice, and I am told that in the gathering season hundreds of bushels of corn are left by the natives untouched in their fields. In some cases American colonists have gone and gathered quantities of it without any payment. Here, then, with an enterprising settlement, corn could be obtained, as an export. The natives, if encouraged, might easily be made vast and extensive corn-growers. This has already taken place on the

---

* Dr. Livingstone saw the cane growing in his tour through South Africa. It is more than probable that that cane is indigenous to both West and South Africa.

Gold Coast. Several cargoes of corn were exported thence in 1859, to England.

As with the palm oil, so with maize, sugar-cane, and cotton; civilized men could, with but little difficulty, increase the cultivation of these articles among the natives, and ship them to traders to their own advantage. And this process is the great secret of West African trade; the foreign merchant, by his goods, excites the cupidity of the simple native who at Fernandapo brings him barwood; at St. Paul Loando, beeswax; at Congo, copal and gutta percha; at Accra, maize; at Cababar, black ebony wood; at Bonny and Lagos, palm oil; at Bassa, (Liberia,) camwood; at Lagos, cotton; at Tantamquerry and Gambra, ground nuts and pepper; at Sierra Leone, nearly *all* kinds of African produce; at Elmina, Cape Coast, Accra, and Bassam, gold. By this multiform traffic, yet, be it remembered, in its infancy, and capable of being increased a thousand-fold, millions of dollars are being made, every year, on the coast of Africa.

Now all this flows into the coffers of white men. I mean nothing invidious by this. I state a fact, and am utterly unconscious of any unworthy or ungenerous feeling, in stating it. "The earth is the Lord's, and the fullness thereof;" and this "fullness" he has given to MAN, irrespective of race or color. The main condition of the obtainment of it is intelligence, forecast, skill, and enterprise. If the black man—the black man, I mean, civilized and enlightened, has lying before him a golden heritage, and fails to seize upon and to appropriate it; Providence, none the less, intends it to be seized upon, and wills it to be used. And if the white man, with a keen eye, a cunning hand, and a wise practicalness, is enabled to appropriate it with skill and effect, it is his; God gives it to him; and he has a right to seek and to search for a multiplication of it; and when he secures it, a right to the use or it,—responsible, however, both to God and man for the use or right means to the ends he has before him, and for the moral features of his traffic.

But while conceding that the white man has, in the main, fairly won the present trade of Africa; I can not but lament over non-participation therein; for the larger advantages of it, go to Europe and America, and help to swell the broad stream of their wealth, luxury, and refinement. And how deep and broad and mighty is that stream, as shown by two facts: 1st, That England, France, and the United States, expend annually more than a million and a half of dollars for the protection of trade on this coast.* And 2d, That the coast swarms with white men, using all possible means and contrivances *to open trade into the interior.* To this one single end, an immense amount of capital is spent by great mercantile houses, in England, France, and America. One single house in Liverpool, employs such a fleet of trading vessels, that it is necessitated to keep a resident physician at the mouth of one of our great rivers for the benefit of their captains and sailors. " A single merchant now living, in the course of three or four years has spent more than $100,000 in exploring the rivers and creeks of Western Africa, merely to ascertain the extent of her commercial relations."† While I am writing these pages, I receive the information that one of the great Liverpool houses, has just sent out a small steamer to the Brights, to collect the oil for their trading vessels. Simultaneously with this intelligence, I am advised that a number of agents are employed by English capitalists to visit the towns from Lagos to Abbeokuta, and to leave with their chiefs, small bags of cotton seed for the growth of cotton. And but a few months ago we hailed in our roads a little fairy craft—the " Sunbeam," steamer sent out by " Laird and Company" for the Niger trade; and since then, I have heard of two of her trips, four hundred miles up that mighty river, bringing thence valuable cargoes from the factories which are now established three hundred miles up upon its banks.

And now perhaps you ask,—" How shall the children of Africa, sojourning in foreign lands, avail themselves of the treasures of this continent?" I answer briefly,—" In the same way white men do." *They* have pointed out the way;

---

* I do not pretend to accuracy in this statement; the expenditure of Great Britain was, in 184-, £231,000.

† Wilson's " Western Africa," pp. 521.

let us follow in the same track and in the use of the like [legitimate] agencies by which trade is facilitated and money is made by them.

Perhaps this is too general; let me therefore attempt something more specific and·distinctive.

FIRST, then, I remark that if individuals are unable to enter upon a trading system, they can form associations. If *one* has not sufficient capital, four or six united can make a good beginning. If a few persons can not make the venture, then a company can be formed. It was in this way the first attempts at trading were made by the Dutch and the English, both in India and Africa. A few men associated themselves together, and sent out their agent or agents, and started a factory. And from such humble beginnings, in the 17th century, has arisen that magnificent Indian Empire, which has helped to swell the vast wealth, and the cumbrous capital of England, from whose arena have come forth such splendid and colossal characters, as Cleve, and Wellington, and Metcalf, and the Laurences, and Havelock; and which has furnished the church of Christ a field on which to display the Apostolic virtues and the primitive self-sacrifice of Middleton, and Heber, and Wilson, of Henry Martyn, of Fox and Ragland.

Without doubt God designs as great things as these for Africa, and among the means and agencies He will employ, commercial enterprise is most certainly one. To this end however, high souls and lofty resolves are necessary, as in any other vocation of life. Of course the timid, the over-cautious, the fearful; men in whose constitution FAITH is a needed quality, are not fitted for this service. If ever the epoch of negro civilization is brought about in Africa; whatever *external* influences may be brought to bear upon this end; whatever foreign agencies and aids, black men themselves are without doubt to be the chief instruments. But they are to be men of force and energy; men who will not suffer themselves to be outrivaled in enterprise and vigor; men who are prepared for pains, and want and suffering; men of such invincible courage that the spirit can not be tamed by transient failures, incidental misadventure, or even glaring miscalculations; men who can exaggerate the feeblest resources into potent agencies and fruitful capital. Moreover these men are to have strong moral proclivities, equal to the deep penetration and the unyielding tenacity of their minds. No greater curse could be entailed upon Africa than the sudden appearance upon her shores, of a mighty host of heartless black buccaneers [for such indeed they would prove themselves ;]— men sharpened up by letters and training ; filled with feverish greed ; with hearts utterly alien from moral good and human well-being ; and only regarding Africa as a convenient goldfield from which to extract emolument and treasure to carry off to foreign quarters.

Such men would only reproduce the worst evils of the last three sad centuries of Africa's history ; and quickly and inevitably so soil their character, that the *just* imputation would be fastened upon them of that malignant lie which has recently been spread abroad through Europe and America against us ; that is, of complicity with the slave trade.*

---

* Nothing can be more judicious than the following words of Commander Foote—"Let then the black man be judged fairly, and not presumed to have become all at once and by miracle, of a higher order than old historic nations, through many generations of whom the political organization of the world has been slowly developing itself. There will be among them men who are covetous, or men who are tyrannical, or men who would sacrifice public interests, or any others to their own ; men who would now go into the slave trade if they could, or rob hen roosts, or intrigue for office, or pick pockets, rather than trouble their heads or their hands with more honorable occupations. It should be remembered by visitors that such things will be found in Liberia ; *not because men are black, but because men are men.*" AFRICA AND THE AMERICAN FLAG, p. 206.

It is most encouraging to find ever and anon a writer who in speaking of colored men avoids the exaggeration of them either into demi-gods or monkeys. Even Commander Foote well nigh loses his balance, on the *same* page whence the above just sentence is taken. In the paragraph which immediately follows this extract, he gives expression to opinions sweepingly disparaging to the negro race, and not of *certain* historical accuracy. Commander Foote says—"*No negro has done anything to lighten or brighten the links of human policy.*" Such a broad assertion implies that the writer has cleared up all the mysteries of past history ; but upon the point, that is, "the relation of Egypt to the negro race," though still a disputed question ; yet, with such authorities on our side as Dr. Pitchard, Cardinal Wiseman and that ripe scholar, the late Alexander H. Everett, one would have supposed Commander Foote would have been a little less venturesome. Moreover, I beg to say that TOUISSANT L'OUVERTURE *is* an historical character. GOODWIN, in his lectures on colonial slavery says : "Can the West India Islands, since

Happily for Africa, most the yearnings of her sons towards her are gentle, humane and generous. When the commercial one shall show itself, it will not differ, I feel assured, from all the others her children have showed. God grant that it may soon burst from many warm and ardent and energetic hearts, for the rescue of a continent!

SECOND. I proceed to show that the whole coast offers facilities for adventurous traders. There are few, if any localities but where they can set up their factories and commence business. If there are exceptions they are rare; and even then, not really such, but cases where at some previous time the natives have been so basely and knavishly treated, that they themselves have learned to practice the same upon some hapless, unsuspecting captain and his crew. As a general thing, however, native African chiefs court and invite the residence of a trader in their neighborhood; will give him protection ; and will strive to secure his permanent stay. On our Liberian coast we see the proof of this in the many factories in existence at divers points. I have myself seen mere boys,—young Englishmen not of age,—who have come out to this country seeking their fortunes, living on the coast in native towns, without any civilized companionship, and carrying on a thriving trade. The chiefs have an interest in these men, and therefore make their residence safe and comfortable. The traders' presence and barter give the King or head-man importance, increase his wealth, augment his influence in the neighborhood, swell the population of his town, and thus make it the center or capital of the surrounding region. But even if it were not thus, the security of traders is insured by the felt power of the three great nations of the civilized world. Such, and so great is the naval force of England, France, and America, on this coast, that the coast may be regarded as protected. The native chiefs, for many hundred

their first discovery by Columbus, boast a single name which deserves comparison with that of Touissant L'Ouverture?" Read Harriet Martineau's "Hour and the man:" Wordsworth's fine Sonnet addressed to "Touissant in prison;" and the noble Poem of John G. Whittier, on the same theme; and then compare the opinions of these high names with Commander Foote's broad assertions.

miles, have been taught to fear the destructive instruments of war they carry with them, and now a days but seldom give occasion for their use.

But aside from all this, I may remark here, 1st, that of all rude and uncivilized men, the native African is the mildest and most gentle; and 2nd, that no people in the world are so given to trade and barter as the negroes of the western coast of Africa.

THIRDLY. Let me refer to the means and facilities colored men have for an entrance upon African commerce. And 1st, I would point out the large amount of capital which is lying in their hands dead and unproductive. There is, as you are doubtless aware, no small amount of wealth possessed by the free colored population of the United States, both North and South. Notwithstanding the multitudinous difficulties which beset them in the pathway of improvement, our brethren have shown capacity, perseverance, oftentimes thrift and acquisitiveness. As a consequence they are, all over the Union, owners of houses, farms, homesteads, and divers other kinds of property; and stored away in safe quarters, they have large amounts of gold and silver; deep down in large stockings, in the corners of old chests, in dark and undiscoverable nooks and crannies; besides larger sums invested in banks, and locked up in the safes of city savings banks.

I have no statistics by me of the population and property of the colored people of Cincinnati, but I am told that their wealth exceeds that of the same class, in any other city in the American Union—that is, according to their numbers. Nashville, Tenn., Charleston, S. C., St. Louis, Mo., Mobile and New Orleans, stand in nearly the same category. Baltimore holds a respectable position. In the "Weekly Anglo-African," (September, 1859,) I find that the CHURCH PROPERTY of the colored population in Philadelphia is put down at $231,484. Doubtless their personal real estate must be worth millions. And the same must be true of New York city.

The greater portion of their wealth, however, is unproductive. As a people we have been victimized in a pecuniary point of view, as well as morally and politically; and as a consequence there is an almost universal dread of entrusting our monies in the hands of capitalists, and trading companies, and stock; though in the great cities large sums are put in savings banks. There are few, however, who have the courage to take shares in railroad and similar companies, and in many places it could not be done.

There is *one* most pregnant fact that will serve to show, somewhat, their monetary ability. "THE AFRICAN METHODIST EPISCOPAL CHURCH" is one of the denominations of the United States. It has its own organization; its own bishops; its conferences, its organ, or magazine; and these entirely *inter se*—absolutely disconnected with all the white denominations of America. This religious body is spread out in hamlet, village, town and city, all through the eastern, northern, western, and (partly) the southern States. But *the* point to which I desire to direct your attention is the fact that they have built and now own some 300 church edifices, mostly brick; and in the large cities, such as New York, Philadelphia and Baltimore, they are large, imposing, capacious, and will seat some two or three thousand people. The free black people of the United States built these churches; the funds were gathered from their small and large congregations; and in some cases they have been known to collect, that is, in Philadelphia and Baltimore, at one collection, over $1,000. The aggregate value of their property can not be less than $5,000,000.

Now this, you will notice, is an exhibit of the corporate monied power of but *one* class of our brethren. I have said nothing about the Episcopal churches, of the Presbyterians, of the Baptists, nor of the divers sections of the Methodists. But this will suffice. You can easily see from the above, that there must be a large amount of pecuniary means in the hands of the free colored population of the American States.

2nd. I turn now to another of their facilities for engaging in African commerce. I refer to NAVIGATION. And here I might rest the case upon the fact that money will purchase vessels, and command seamen and navigators. But you already have *both*. Turn for a moment to New Bedford, Mass. It is now some twenty years since I visited that important seaport. Though but a boy, I kept my eyes open, especially upon the condition of our race there; and I retain still a vivid remembrance of the signs of industry and thrift among them, of the evidences of their unusual wealth, and of their large interest in shipping. I had the names of several parties mentioned to me who were owners of whale craft, and I made the acquaintance of some of them. Among these I remember well some youthful descendants of Paul Cuffee. The same state of things, I apprehend exists, though perhaps in a much less degree, in some places in Connecticut; on the Hudson, that is, at Albany and Newburgh, in the State of New York ; on the Potomac; at St. Louis, on the Mississippi, and on the Red River. There are scores, if not hundreds of colored men who own schooners, and other small craft in those localities ; pilots and engineers, captains and seamen, who, if once moved with a generous impulse to redeem the land of their fathers, could, in a brief time, form a vast commercial marine, equal to all the necessities of such a glorious project.

Let me dwell for a moment upon one suggestion, that is, the facilities for securing seamen, and the comparative ease of forming crews. Colored seamen, in large numbers, I apprehend, can easily be obtained. Even in the United States their numbers are legion ; and we may proudly say that, in activity, dutifulness and skill, they are equal to any sailors on the globe. Nor would there be any great lack of the needed class just above the grade of sailors, that is, a class who would join intelligence and knowledge to practicalness. What a number of men, trained to a late boyhood in the colored schools, do we not know who have sailed for years out of New York as "stewards" in the great "liners" ! How many of these are there not, who both at school and by experience, have attained a real scientific acquaintance with navigation. And how many of them, had they been white men, would long ere this, have risen to the posts of mates and captains! How many of such could you and I point out, who were our school-mates, in the old " free school," in Mulberry street ! *

---

* In a most elaborate paper, entitled " THE NIGER TRADE," by Sir George Stephen, (Simpkin, Marshall & Co., London, 1849,) the author shows, most

Here, then, you have the material and the designated agency for an almost boundless commercial staff, for the purposes of trade in West Africa. The facts I have adduced can not, I think, be disputed. And on the condition that this machinery is brought into operation, the influences and results are easily anticipated. It must follow, as a necessity, that the trade and commerce of Africa shall fall into the hands of black men. At an early day whole fleets of vessels, manned and officered by black men from the United States and Liberia, would outrival all the other agencies which are now being used for grasping West African commerce. Large and important houses would spring into existence among you, all through the states. Wealth would flow into your coffers, and affluence would soon exhibit itself amid all your associations. The reproach of penury and the consciousness of impotency in all your relations would rapidly depart. And as a people you would soon be able to make yourselves a felt element of society in all the relations of life, on the soil where you were born.

These are some of the *material* influences which would result from this movement. The moral and philanthropic results would be equally if not more notable. The kings and tradesmen of Africa, having the *demonstration* of negro capacity before them, would hail the presence of their black kinsmen from America,* and would be stimulated to a generous emulation. To the farthest interior, leagues and combinations would be formed with the men of commerce, and thus civilization, enlightenment and Christianity would be carried to every state, and town, and village of interior Africa. The

clearly, the need and the practicability of employing the agency of black men, for the purposes of African civilization. Sir George suggested the employment of them, in the [British] naval as well as merchant service; in all grades of office, from seamen and marines up to naval officers; and he points to the West India Colonies, and Hayti, remarking, " Hayti has a navy exceeding twenty in number, of which four are steamers; all are, of course, manned and officered by black or colored men." In this paper, Sir George quotes and emphasises the words of Mc-Queen—" *It is by African hands and African exertions chiefly that the evil must be rooted out.*"

* Just this has been the experience of Dr. Delany, as I hear from valued friends there, at Lagos, and other places.

4

galling remembrances of the slave trade on the coast, and of slavery in America, would quicken the blood and the brain of both parties; and every wretch of a slave trader who might visit the coast, would have to atone for his temerity by submitting to the rigid code framed for piracy. And when *this* disturbing and destructive hindrance to African progress was once put down, noble cities, vast agricultural establishments, the seeds of universities, and ground-work of church organizations, would spring up all along the banks, and up the valley of the Niger.*

There is one certain commercial result—to return to my subject—that would surely grow out of this movement; I mean the flow of large amounts of capital from the monied men of America, that is, if black men showed skill, energy and practicability. Philanthropy would come forward with largess for colored men, thus developing the resources of Africa. Religion would open a large and generous hand in order to hasten the redemption of a continent, alien from Christ and His church. And capital would hasten forward, not only for its wonted reduplication, but also to exemplify the vitality and fruitfulness which it always scatters from golden hands in its open pathway. And when you consider the fact of kinship, on our part, with Africa, the less liability to fever, the incentive to gain, the magnificent objects before us, and the magnificent field on which to develop them, and the probable early power of intelligent black men to penetrate, scathless, any neighborhood where they might reside, you can see the likelihood of an early repossession of Africa, in trade, commerce, and moral power, by her now scattered children, in distant lands.

For the carrying out such a plan you have, I repeat myself, you have almost, if not quite, all the needed means and agencies, even now, at hand. You have, all through the states, men who can at once furnish the capital for the commencement of such a venture. You know I am not wont to exaggerate the wealth of colored men. In such matters I prefer

---

* The great hindrance to African evangelization at the present time is the slave trade. Missionaries feel this all along the coast, from Cape Palmas to Congo.

fact to conjecture ; for certainly among us on this subject, imagination has too often proved " a forward and delusive faculty." Yet I do know of some of our brethren in the States who have become monied men,—not millionaires indeed, but men worth their thousands. Some of these men are more prominent individuals than others, and as their names are not unfrequently mentioned in such a connection as this, it may not seem invidious in a like mention on these pages. Some of these persons are acquaintances—a few, old friends of former years, but the most are personally unknown to me. There are Rev. Stephen Smith, William Whipper, Esq., of Philadelphia; Messrs. Knight & Smith, of Chicago, Ill.; Messrs. Cook & Moxly, of Buffalo, N. Y. ; Youngs & Wilcox, of Cincinnati, &c., &c.

It is possible that in a few instances earnest prejudice against everything African may cause displeasure at this designation. Any one can see that I have intended nothing discourteous ; and it should be remembered that commercial enterprise in Africa has no necessary connection with emigration, or colonization. How great soever the diversities of opinion upon these points, on *this* platform Douglass and Delany can stand beside the foremost citizens and merchants of Liberia. Hence those men whose feelings are the most averse to anything like colonization, can not object to the promotion of trade and the acquisition of wealth. Indeed, I have no doubt that there are thousands who would be glad of a safe investment in anything wherein there is probability of advantage. Moreover the fretted mind of our brethren needs distraction from griefs and the causes of grief. Just now, when darkness shrouds their Southron heavens, what could be more opportune, what more desirable than such a movement. The danger is that thousands of them, in their sorrows, may sit down, hopeless, careless, and

> "——Nurse despair
> And feed the dreadful appetite of death."

Your leading men should strive to occupy the vacant minds of their despairing brethren by the healthful stimulant of duty and enterprise.

Doubtless there are many persons in the States who will view the above suggestions in connection with the Liberian Republic, and in my opinion it will be wise and judicious for them so to do. I have nothing extravagant to say about Liberia. It is a theme upon which I never fall into ecstacies. I can not find in it as yet place or occasion for violent raptures. I get started a little, at times, from cool equanimity, when I read the wonderful tales of travelers about the country, or the first letters of enthusiastic settlers. Liberia is a young country, hardly yet "in the gristle,"—laying, as I dare to affirm, good foundations, but with much pain, great trials, consuming anxieties, and with the price of great tribulation, and much mortality. But is not this the history of all young countries? Has not God married pain and suffering and death, to the fresh beginnings of all new nationalities? Would it not be marvelous, not; to say miraculous, if it were true, that the history of *this* colony—for it is nothing more than a colony as yet—that it had been exempted from these trials? And what right have we to expect that God, in these days, will work miracles, especially for black men?*

I have never been disappointed in anything moral, social or political that I have met with in this land. I came to the country expecting all the peculiarities of struggling colonial life, with the added phase of imported habits, tinctured with the deterioration, the indifference, the unthriftiness, which are gendered by *any* servile system. "All work is badly done by people in despair," says Pliny the naturalist.† A forty days' passage through the deep sea can not effect such a regenerating influence as to alter character, and to implant hope,

---

* "No new country can be founded unless under the greatest difficulties. It is the universal law of experience, that however in the late stages of their existence colonies may be prosperous, and to what state soever they may have advanced in the accumulation of wealth, their infant life must always be a life of difficulty and peril."—*Rt. Hon. W. E. Gladstone, Speech before Propagation Soc., Liverpool,* 1858.

† Lord Bacon discourses most pertinently and powerfully to the same effect. See Art. 33 of *"Plantations," "Bacon's Essays and Wisdom of the Ancients."* I regret I can not copy the whole of it here.

ambition, thrift, order, and perseverance, where they have never been cultivated.

These anticipations proved correct, save that I found a stronger and a more general disposition to labor than the sad history of our brethren warranted my looking for.* Many things gratified me from the first. Since then Liberia has grown much. Development shows itself on every side. The acquisition principle manifests itself, and in less than ten years large fortunes will be made; extensive farms spring up; ships be built on our rivers and sail to Europe and America. There is every sign, too, that the springs of trade will shortly, through our own direct influence, be started through all our native population, for 200 miles in the interior; and that this trade will be our own; and that it will originate a commerce excelling that of Sierra Leone. I believe verily that the great principles of industry, of thrift, and expansion are daily taking deeper root in the soil; and that ultimately they will outgrow and exclude all the weeds of lazy self-content, inflated and exaggerated vanity, unthrift, and extravagance. Of course we have here stupid obstructions, men who cling tenaciously to the " dead past;" a few millinered and epauleted gentry,

---

* The people of Liberia are not lazy, although I am sorry to say, *appearances* are sometimes against them. The case is this :—*Many new men do not know how to labor for* THEMSELVES ! They come, at a mature age, when their habits are fixed, into a new school, the operations of which they are unacquainted with. They go into the "bush," and its formidableness overcomes, and crushes them ; they sit down in despair and do nothing, and many perish. "Are not such men lazy?" asks some objector. I say no! and my reason for saying so is this : In the year 1856 there were scores of the class above described on the St. Paul's river, doing nothing. Some four or five farmers commenced the cultivation of sugar cane and the manufacture of sugar. This new effort required large numbers of laborers, and as soon as the need was known, the river was alive with men seeking labor. *Who* were these men ? The hopeless, the despairing men, who could not see their way through the "bush," and could not improve their own farmsteads. I have seen scores of these men trudging through the rain and mud, in the rainy season, or paddling in fragile canoes, seeking the larger plantations, clamorous for labor ; and I have seen the supply so great that a *dozen* men had to be refused at a time. Why was this ? These men had been unaccustomed to self support. Placed under a proprietor, heart and limb were alive with an industrious impulse. Liberia needs CAPITALISTS who can employ this large class of men. Mr. RUFFIN, of Virginia, will perhaps claim this as a proof that black men must have masters. Students of " Political Economy " will put it among the facts which show that where capital languishes, men die, both in body and soul,

"——Neat and trimly dressed,
And fresh as bridegrooms,"

who would civilize our heathen neighbors with powder and shot; and a few unthinking, unreasoning men, who verily believe that the foundations of all great states have been laid in barter and pelf. But these are by no means the *representative* men of the land. If they were, I should despair of any future for Liberia, and depart.

We have another, a larger class than these; a class which comprises awakened old men, and generous and ardent youth; the minds, whose great object in life is not mere gain, or comfort; but who feel that they have a great work to accomplish for their children, for their race, and for God; who feel that they have been called to this mission, and who wish to spend themselves in the expansion and compacting of this youthful republic, to save bleeding, benighted Africa, and to help redeem the continent. I assure you that there is a school of this character in Liberia; men who feel obligated to philanthropy, who are burdened with a sense of duty; who have the keenest, most sensitive feeling of race, who love Africa, who are anxious for the welfare of the whole negro family, who labor with all their might for the advancement of industry and civilization, who would fain glorify God. When I look upon this class of men, and mark their ways, I feel that the country will yet attain standing and reach some distinction.*

It is these thoughts and observations, and some experiences,

---

* I can not better illustrate the importance of such a class, as above mentioned, in Liberia, than by referring to a paragraph from a speech recently sent me by a friend: "If the founders of the American Republic had been formed by the same materials as the settlers of California, the genius and liberties of America would have been lost in anarchy or absorbed in an inevitable despotism. It was because, on however small a scale, they were senators and soldiers, impressed with a due sense of the heavy responsibility that rested upon them, and not mere money-getters, that they succeeded in laying the foundations of the greatest republic in the world. They never lost sight of the responsibility of the task they had undertaken,—they felt that they were going for a high position in the eyes of the world, and to set an example for all ages. Feeling this, the early settlers of New England accomplished their mission."

JOHN ROBERT GODLY, Esq.,
before the " Canterbury Association," London.

which lead me to think that those who look upon Liberia in connection with their commercial desires, are wise. I have no wish to discourage those who are looking to the banks of the Niger. God bless them, every way, if that is indeed their mission! But, as an individual, I have earnestly desired a non-sanguinary evangelization of West Africa. All empire, the world over, in rude countries, has been cemented by blood. In Western Africa the tribes, universally, save in Liberia, are strong, independent, warlike. Even British prowess, both at Sierra Leone, and on the Gold coast, succumbs, at times, to their indomitable spirit. And thus you see that for the establishment of a strong black civilization in central Africa, a strong and a bloody hand must be used. Color is nothing, anywhere. Civilized *condition* differences men, all over the globe. Besides this, I have had a prejudice that *that* field God had given to the freed and cultivated men of Sierra Leone,—that they were better fitted to the evangelization of the Niger than we; that we, with our peculiarities, bred amid American institutions, might prove a disturbing element to the great work, for which, by blood, training, lingual capacity, and the sympathy of character and habits, they were peculiarly fitted; and that our governmental proclivities might jar with what seems a manifest providence, that is, that christianity is to be engrafted upon such strong states as Dahomey and Ashantee; whose fundamental *governmental* basis, it seems to me, it is not for the interests of civilization and of Africa to revolutionize or to disturb.

I would not pretend to argue these points, much less to dogmatise upon them; for the need of a civilizing element at LAGOS, especially, at Abbeokuta, and on the Niger, is so great that I fear even to state the above impressions. And I stand ready to hail, at any time, any nucleus of freedom and enlightenment that may spring up anywhere on the coast of Africa.

In Liberia, we have the noblest opportunities and the greatest advantages. We have a rich and varied soil,—inferior, I verily believe, to but few, if any, on the globe. We have some of the proofs, and many of the indications of varied and vast mineral wealth of the richest qualities. We have a country finely watered in every section by multitudinous brooks and streams, and far-reaching rivers. We have a climate which needs but be educated and civilized and tempered by the plastic and curative processes of emigration, clearances and scientific farming, to be made as fine and as temperate as any land in the tropics can be.

On this soil have been laid the foundations of Republican Institutions. Our religion is Protestant, with its characteristic tendencies to freedom, progress and human well-being. We are reaching forward as far as a young and poor nation can, to a system of common schools. Civilization, that is, in its more simple forms, has displaced ancestral paganism in many sections of the land, has taken permanent foothold in our territory, and already extended its roots among our heathen kin. Our heathen population, moreover, in the immediate neighborhood of our settlements, is but small and sparse; thus saving our civilization from too strong an antagonism, and allowing it room, scope and opportunity for a hardy growth in its more early days. Active industry is now exhibiting unwonted vigor, and begins to tell upon commerce and the foreign market.

Now when you consider that all these elements, humble, as indeed they are, are our own; that we are the creature and dependent of no foreign government; you will agree with me, I think, that men who have families will act wisely in looking narrowly at our advantages, ere they place themselves in circumstances where the moral elements of life and society are more rude, and where the formation agency and influence will belong to some foreign power. That these elements are slow in growth and expansion is true; but this, it will be remembered, furnishes probability of their being sure and permanent.

I have heard the poverty of our particular locality contrasted with the richness of other parts of West Africa. Well, this may be the case; but I think there can be no doubt that there is no nobler, more commanding position in West Africa, than that of Liberia. We hold, I think, the key to the vast interior. You have heard it said, and seen it published, that we have no great rivers. But the St. Paul's, the Booma,* the St. John's, and the Cavalla rivers, stretch away into the far interior 300 and 400 miles, with great breadth, and with a vast volume of water. That they come from the same great water-shed from whence, on an opposite side the Niger drains its mighty waters, seems almost a certainty. And if so, the valley of the Niger, with its wondrous resources, and its teeming wealth, will, ultimately, be as available to us as any other people. At present, these rivers are not navigable any great distance, owing to falls and rapids. But black men in Africa must do what enterprising men do in all other new lands; they must BEND NATURE TO THEIR WANTS AND WISHES. Ship canals are needed twenty miles from the coast, around the rapids of the St. Pauls, and eighty miles from the coast around the falls of the Cavalla; and ship canals must therefore be made. If we have not the *means*, we must go to work and acquire them. If we have not the *science* and the *skill*, we must form our schools and colleges, and put our sons in the way of learning them. And if we have not the men, that is, the *population*, for such a vast and laborious undertaking, we must lift up a loud voice, and call upon hopeful, vigorous, intelligent and energetic black men, all over the globe, "Ho to the rescue!" "Come over and help us!"

And these are just the great needs of Liberia:—men, learning, and wealth. And wealth, here, as an acquisition, requires the use of the same means, and is regulated by the same laws, as in any other land. It requires forecast, wakefulness, industry, thrift, probity, and tireless, sweatful toil; as well in tropical Africa, as in cold Holland. There is no royal road to the soil.

—— "Nil nisi magno
Vita labore dedit mortalibus."

As to *learning*, we have no greater need than this *save* ~~same~~

---

* The BOOMA is a river at Cape Mt. Settlement. I heard that it is the greatest river in Liberia. I am just informed, as this paper leaves me, that an acquaintance has ascended it, some 90 miles, without any obstruction.

religion; and there can be no excess of means, no superabundance of agencies, no delicacy or profundity of culture, unadapted to actual present needs of all this wide region of Liberia. We have our native population, and we have our emigrant youth and children—thousands upon thousands, all around us. And when I look at the quickness, the capacity, and the thirst of the nations for enlightenment, I can see no difference in the needs of one from the other ; I regard them in the general, as our intellectual equals. If I anticipated for them a merely *secular* training, I should prefer a difference; but feeling, knowing that the Chistian religion is to mould, and fashion, and leaven everything here in future times, I go for the highest culture that can be given the rising generation, and hail every facility for the furtherance of this end, which providence grants us. In the first passage of the heathen from barbarism it will doubtless be advisable to make much of their training, physical, and to be content with the Bible and moral instruction ; but the ultimate aim should be, and most surely will be here, to open to them all the broad avenues of instruction and culture. The great cause of apprehension, just now is, that the means for supplying general education are but partial ; and that the actual need created by our circumstances, for the attainment of good literary and scientific training can not be obtained.

* I come to population. We *need* immigration. We are poor in men and women. We do not number over 14,000 emigrant citizens. Numbers of these are crippled, I mean in soul more than body, ere they come here. The poverty of emigrants dwarfs the otherwise actual force of the country ; and old age, in both sexes, and especially the fact that a large per centage of emigrants are helpless females with children, without husbands, brings out the sad truth that our real available man-force is but small. And yet the moral calls upon us in this new sphere, the intellectual demands, and the physical requirements, with the vastness of territory, and the largeness of providential circumstances around us, while they quicken imagination, fix also the conviction of helpless weakness ; and in some men produce indifference or despair ; in

others, vexation and painful anxiousness. The population question is dwarfing the powers of our strong and earnest leaders. They can not lift themselves up to grand ideas, and large conceptions. In all their efforts they are " cribbed, cabined and confined."

We need this day for the great work before us, in a region of not less than 500,000 square miles; we need, I say, not less than 50,000 *civilized men*. We ought to be traveling onward through the land ; and to appropriate and modify a remark of De Toquevillés—to be " peopling our vast wilderness at the average rate of at least five miles per annum." And for the work of civilization and enlightenment among our aboriginal population, we should have even now, a mental power and a moral force working through all our territory, fitted for just such a transformation as has been produced in New Zealand and the Sandwich Islands, in a period of twenty-five years. The tide of immigration, as it now sets in, promises us no such results. Our ratio of increase, with our present diverse disturbing influences, is but small. Unfortunately there is no general consciousness of our lack and need in this respect. I have had the fear that some of my fellow-citizens accustomed themselves to look upon Liberia as a "close corporation." The attempt to pass a " naturalization law," in the face of the fact that it takes YEARS to add a thousand living men to our population, chiefly caused that fear. But we, in common with you, are becoming awake to the conviction that, *as a race*, we have a great work to do. The zeal of England and of America, for Africa, is opening our eyes. Our own thoughtful men begin to feel the binding tie which joins them in every interest and feeling, with the negro race, all over the globe. Your " Anglo-African Magazines," " Douglas' Journal," and patriotic addresses begin to tell upon us. And soon there will be a kindled eye, a quickened pulse, a beating heart, and large and generous emotions, for our bruised and wounded brethren everywhere. And when that day comes the people of Liberia will cry out:— "*We* have the largest advantages of all our race. We have the noblest field. Ours is the most signal providence ; and our State offers the grandest possibilities of good, the finest opportunities of manly achievement. Why then suffer ourselves to be hindered in working out of ' manifest destinies ' of beneficence to suffering Africa by the narrowness of our aims, or the fewness of our numbers and means? It is true we have a wide field to enter, and need more and mightier men to enter it. Let us therefore call our skillful and enegetic brethren to come to us and share the suffering and the glory of saving Africa. Let us stand on the beach and on the hill-side, and beckon to them in ALL LANDS to come and participate in lofty duty—in painful but saving labor, and to aid in the restoration and enlightenment of a vast continent ! ''

I turn now to the *religious* aspect of this subject. In speaking of the religious needs of Africa, it is not necessary I should attempt a picture of her miserable condition, nor enter into the details of her wretchedness. Her very name is suggestive of uttermost spiritual need ; of abounding moral desolation ; of the deepest, darkest ignorance ; of wild and sanguinary superstitions. This whole continent, with its million-masses of heathen, presents one broad, almost unbroken, unmitigated view of moral desolation and spiritual ruin. And this fact creates the demand upon the Christian world for ministers and teachers, for the purpose of her evangelization. '' The field is the world,'' and the church is to occupy it; and she will occupy it.

As members of the church of Christ, the sons of Africa in foreign lands are called upon to bear their part in the vast and sacred work of her evangelization. I might press this point on the grounds of piety, of compassion, or sympathy, but I choose a higher principle. For next to the grand ideas which pertain to the Infinite, His attributes and perfections, there is none loftier and grander than that of DUTY—

"Stern daughter of the voice of God."

It is the duty of black men to feel and labor for the salvation of the mighty millions of their kin all through this continent. I know that there is a class of her children who repudiate any close and peculiar connection with Africa. They and their fathers have been absent from this soil for centuries. In the course of time their blood has been mingled somewhat with that of other peoples and races. They have been brought up and habituated to customs entirely diverse from those of their ancestors in this land. And while the race here are in barbarism, they, on the other hand, are civilized and enlightened.

But notwithstanding these pleas there are other great facts which grapple hold of these men, and bind them to this darkened, wretched negro race, by indissoluble bonds. There is the fact of kinship, which a lofty manhood and a proud generosity keeps them now, and ever will keep them from disclaiming. There are the strong currents of kindred blood which neither time nor circumstance can ever entirely wash out. There are the bitter memories of ancestral wrongs, of hereditary servitude, which can not be forgotten till " the last syllable of recorded time." There is the bitter pressure of legal proscription, and of inveterate caste, which will crowd closer and closer their ranks, deepening brotherhood and sympathy, and preserving, vital, the deep consciousness of distinctive race. There still remains the low imputation of negro inferiority, necessitating a protracted and an earnest battle, creative of a generous pride to vindicate the race, and inciting to noble endeavor to illustrate its virtues and its genius.

How then can these men ever forget Africa? How cut the links which bind them to the land of their fathers? I affirm therefore that it is the duty of black men, in foreign lands, to live and to labor for the evangelization of the land of their fathers: 1st, on the ground of humanity ; 2d, because they themselves are negroes, or the descendants of negroes, and are measurably responsible to God for the salvation of their heathen kin ; and 3dly, I press the consideration of duty on the ground that they are Christians. In the good providence of God they have been enabled to pass out of the spiritual benightedness of their fathers, into the high table lands and the divine atmosphere of Christian truth and Christian conviction.

Now I shall not attempt any *formal* argument in proof that black men [or, to use the new term,] Anglo-Africans are duty bound to extend the gospel in Africa ; for I know enough of human nature to see that such an argument would look like the assumption that our brethren in the States were so ignorant that they did not know their duty as Christians. The very men who, perchance, would contest every other point in this letter, would charge me with insult, if I had just here put forth an *argument to prove* that Christianity requires *black* Christians to be missionaries as well as white ones. They would start up and exclaim : "Do you think that we read our Bibles and yet remain ignorant of the evangelizing spirit of the Bible ? Do you think that we are such fools as to suppose that the precepts and commands of scripture have a *color* on them ? And do you suppose that we are such ignorant creatures, that you must needs present an argument to prove to us that we should manifest a missionary heart as well as other Christians ? We do not need your teachings, sir. We know something about Christianity as well as you."

I attempt no such argument. It is not to be supposed for a moment, that black Christians in New York, Philadelphia and Baltimore, do not know that there are no distinctions in Christian requirement, that her obligations are as weighty upon them as upon any portion of the church. I am only endeavoring to show that while that portion of the race that lives in America, owes duty in America, it has obligations which likewise pertain to Africa; that devotedness to the cause of the black man in the United States, does not necessarily exclude sympathy for Africa. Let me illustrate this. There is a phase of modern theological writing, which brings out most prominently the fact that our Lord Jesus Christ, though born of a Jewish mother, shows no where Jewish idiosyncracies. You look at the Lord Jesus, you read his life, you study his words, and no where can you discover nationality. Men of every clime and blood and nation turn to Him, and they find each and all in Him, the reflex of one common broad humanity.

The Apostle, St. Paul, more than any other mere man,

reached the nearest to this grand and divine Catholicity of the Master. "I am debtor both to the Greeks and to the Barbarians: both to the wise and to the unwise. So, as much as in me is, I am ready to preach the Gospel to you that are at Rome also." Romans, Chapter i, 14, 15.

Nay, he went even beyond this. In his Epistle to the Thessalonians he speaks of his kinsmen the Jews, in a way which would lead one to suppose that he had become thoroughly denationalized. "For ye also have suffered like things of your own countrymen, even as they have of the Jews: Who both killed the Lord Jesus, and their own prophets, and have persecuted us; and they please not God, and are contrary to all men." 1 Thessalonians, ii, 14, 15. So thoroughly had the grace of God eliminated from the soul of St. Paul, that withering and malignant principle of caste, which burned more fiercely and intensely in the Jewish mind and blood, than in any other people that ever lived.

And yet, look at this same large-hearted, Catholic-minded Paul; what a patriot he is! what longings he has for his race! How he falls back upon their high and noble prerogatives! Yea, what zeal, what deep desire, what earnest self-sacrifice he cherishes for them! "What advantage hath the Jew?" he asks, "Or what profit is there of circumcision? Much every way: chiefly because that unto them were committed the oracles of God." Romans, iii, 1, 2. The Epistle to the Romans was written after that to the Thessalonians. And again, in the 9th chapter. He says,—"I say the truth in Christ, I lie not, my conscience also bearing me witness in the Holy Ghost, that I have great heaviness and continual sorrow in my heart. For I could wish that myself were accursed from Christ for my brethren, my kinsmen according to the flesh: who are Israelites, to whom pertaineth the adoption, and the glory, and the covenants, and the giving of the law, and the service of God and the promises; whose are the fathers, and of whom as concerning the flesh Christ came, who is over all, God blessed for ever. Amen."

To be Catholic minded then does not imply a lack of patriotism. Large, yea cosmopolitan views, do not necessarily demand a sacrifice of kinship, a disregard of race, nor a spirit of denationality.

Even so our brethren in the United States; however manfully they claim citizenship in the land of their birth; however valiantly, against all odds they stand beside their brethren in bonds ; however nobly they may continue to battle for their rights ; need not, nevertheless feel less for the hundreds of millions of their kin " without God and without hope in the world," " in bondage to sin and Satan ;" nor yet to put forth less generous effort for their well-being and eternal salvation.

I turn from the point of *duty* to the question of your *ability* and *power* to take part in this great work. I do not know whether or not, colored men in the United States would generally acknowledge that they could as a people do something for Africa ; I assume, however, as most probable, the affirmative. At the same time I must say that I do not think there is any deep conviction of either the awful needs of the case, or the solemn obligations connected with it.

I see however, that this very question of your ability is both questioned and denied in some quarters. I see in the " Spirit of Missions " [October, 1858,] a report of a speech of Rev. Dr. I. Leighton Wilson, secretary of the Presbyterian Board of Missions, which is of this tenor. He says—" To withdraw our Missionaries, is virtually to consign those people to perpetual and unmitigated heathenism. The speaker knew of no substitute for the present plan of Missionary operation. In the colonization scheme, he entertained the liveliest interest. The Liberian Republic offers a comfortable home for those in the United States who choose to go there, but it can never exert an influence which will reach the remote part of the continent. To study out the barbarous languages—prepare dictionaries—to give shape to a community emerging into the light of civilization—we never look to colored men as best adapted to this work. We were shut up to the conclusion that we must pursue this work in the manner already commenced."

I regret exceedingly that one who has done and suffered so much for Africa, as Dr. Wilson has, should have ventured such disparaging remarks concerning any of her children as the above.* For if he had put himself to the pains of inquiring into the capacity of the "colored men around him," he would never, I feel convinced, have thus spoken. I am no more disposed to exaggerate the learning or mental ability of our race than their wealth. Indeed, as a race, there is no place for exaggeration. As yet, we are but " parvenus " in the intellectual world. Our greatness lies in the future, as yet we have not secured. Nevertheless American black men have done, and are now doing enough to challenge respect. And even that seems to be withheld by Dr. Wilson ; possibly I may mistake him. But when American black men are ably editing literary journals, publishing respectable newspapers, issuing from the press volumes of sermons, writing scientific disquisitions, venturing abstruse " Theories of Comets," and sending forth profound " vital statistics," vexatious alike to opposing Statesmen and Divines ; they so far vindicate their mental power and ability, as to make it manifest, that, under better circumstances, in a clear field, they could

—"Move and act
In all the correspondences of nature,"

with force, and skill, and effect.

But Dr. Wilson knows nothing of this particular class of black men. He and hundreds like him know nothing of them. And this is one of the original signs of the deadly power of caste. It victimizes the white as well as the black man. Here is mind,—active struggling mind—developing itself under most interesting circumstances ; rising above the depression of centuries ; breaking away from ancestral benightedness and hereditary night ; gradually gathering strength, and emerging into light ; and at length securing respectability and attracting attention, and yet if this phenomenon, which excited the admiration of Dr. Channing, and arrested the attention of Lord Carlyle and Dr. Playfair, passing travelers,

---

* It is hardly necessary for me to tell you that Dr. Wilson has spent the flower of his years on this coast in self sacrifice for Africa ; nor to add that it was *chiefly* through a rigorous and timely pamphlet of his that the British Squadron was not withdrawn from this coast in 1851.

Dr. Wilson apparently knows nothing of, but actually speaks slightingly of.

Dr. Wilson rejects the idea of your being capable of exerting a remote and extensive influence. I beg to point out his error by a reference again to the " African Methodist Church," in the United States. I make this reference on the ground that in the church of God " there are diversities of gifts, but the same spirit ;" and " there are differences of administrations, but the same Lord ;" and " that the manifestation of the spirit is given to every man to profit withal ;" and yet again, that in the great work of Christ for the salvation of the heathen, even *those very " members of the body* [of Christ] *which seem to be more feeble, are necessary.*"*

And, while fully agreeing to the affirmation more distinctly stated by Dr. Wilson than I have ever seen it expressed before, that, " the idea of gathering up colored men indiscriminately, and setting them down upon the shores of Africa, with the design or expectation that they will take the lead in diffusing a pure Christianity among the nations, deserves to be utterly rejected by every friend of Africa."† Still it seems to me that he commits an error similar to that of rejecting the light artillery of an army, because the " cavalry " is a stronger arm of it.

Doubtless *all* the religious societies of colored people in America are humble, that is as it respects literary and theological qualifications; and the African Methodist Church as much as any other. I do not think they themselves would make any pretensions. *But have they fitness for practical usefulness ?* We can only determine this by facts. Now this denomination has been in existence since 1790. It has gathered into its fold tens of thousands of the sons of Africa on American soil.

" The poor forsaken ones : "

Men however of earnest mind, who would not sit in the " negro pew ; men, who but for this society must have been

---

* 1 Corinthians xii : 5, 6, 7,—22.
† Wilson's " Western Africa," p. 507.

left to indifferentism or infidelity, have had their wounded hearts soothed by the visitations of this society, and their anxious passionate gaze turned from the trials of caste and slavery, to "the Lamb of God, who taketh away the sin of the world." They have built churches, established schools, founded a college, raised up a ministry of over four hundred men, meet in several conferences, and are governed by their own bishops. Here then is a spiritual machinery which has saved the United States the shame of hundred of thousands black heathen. Where is a purely missionary enterprise in the full tide of success, which has been administered by black men over a half century—stretching from Maine to Louisiana, from Maryland to California; it shows that black men " *can exert an influence which will reach the remote part of the continent* " of America; and why not do the same on the continent of Africa ? Operating among negroes, most of whom a century ago were recently from Africa; it shows that American Christians, even *now*, " *can look to colored men as* " [at least, *humbly*] " *adapted to the work*," that is " *to give shape to a community emerging into the light of civilization*." The disproof of Dr. Wilson's assertion is right before his eyes.

Dr. Wilson's objection, that we are " not best adapted to study out the barbarous languages and prepare dictionaries," I regard as exceedingly unfair. There is not a missionary society in Christendom whose choice of missionaries is conditioned on this single qualification—their " ability to study barbarous languages and prepare dictionaries ! " It strikes too as much against *white* missionaries *abroad* as against black men ; for are they " BEST ADAPTED," in these respects, compared with such distinguished divines and scholars as Dr. Robinson, Dr. Goodrich, Dr. Turner ? Besides how many dictionaries have the fishermen of Galilee transmitted to modern times ? What evidence have we of an eminent scholarship among them like to this demanded of us ? Or where is the proof that even the Holy Spirit regarded " the preparation of dictionaries," or a critical lingual capacity as *the* qualifications of missionaries ?

We read the history of the church, and see the conquests of the faith in ancient times in Europe, Asia, and Africa. But how rare a thing is it, to find such pre-eminent scholarships as, for instance, that of Henry Martyn, Bishop Middleton, and David Tappan Stoddard, the accessories of the devoted missionary spirit, which has converted millions, and brought whole nations into the kingdom of Christ. St. Paul founded the churches of Asia and Greece. But where is the proof that even he was an eminent critical scholar? Christianity was revived and energized in England by Augustine in the 6th century, and then traveled onward with conquering power, until the time of the reformation; and since then the evangelization of England has been progressing with a resistless march to the present. But the first English dictionary we know of is that of Dr. Johnson.

If I do not mistake the spirit of the New Testament, it requires, I apprehend, in addition to devoted piety, good sterling qualities, and an "aptness to teach," as the ordinary gifts of ministers: [and what are missionaries but ministers?] It can not go below this standard; but it may rise above it to the fiery zeal and wasting labors of St. Paul; the effective eloquence of Xavier, and Swartz, and Brainerd; the fine abilities and practical learning of Carey and Medhurst.

If to ordinary gifts, missionaries are able to add these other eminent ones, so much the better fitted will they be to make skillful and effective workers in the Lord's vineyard!

But if not, then missionaries, that is, colored missionaries, to Africa, must be content to labor as effectively as they can, without them; relying for translations and the superior literary work of missions, upon the occasional white laborers who come from abroad. And with respect to the languages, they must do as two-thirds, not to say three-fourths, of the white missionaries do, that is, work for the heathen through the agency of interpreters. In Liberia, however, more than a *third*, not to say *half*, of the colored ministers, speak the respective native tongues in their vicinity, with ease; and of candidates for the ministry, in the different denominations, I feel well nigh confident that four-fifths of them speak one or two *native* tongues.

You have then humble QUALIFICATIONS fitted to make you, although not learned, yet useful and effective instruments in the salvation of our heathen kin. You can become preachers and teachers; and the more learned labor can be done by white brethren. As you have fitness, so likewise you have the OPPORTUNITY to enter upon this glorious and saving work. I wish to show here that if you love Africa, and really possess a missionary spirit, the way is open before you to enter at once among the crowded populations of this continent, and to set up the standard of the Cross. From the port of Lagos in almost direct line through a crowded population, and passing by cities containing tens of thousands of people, a highway is now open reaching to RABBA on the banks of the Niger. All through this country the colored churches of America can send their missionaries, build up Christian schools, and lay the foundation of Christian colleges and universities. North of us lies the wide and open field of the Mendians, which is the door to the mighty millions of interior Africa, back to Timbuctoo. Between these two fields of labor is the republic of Liberia. Our name, our reputation, and our flag, will insure you safety two hundred miles from the coast, among large, important, industrious, and active-minded natives. It was only the other day that I made a second visit to an interior station, in company with Dr. Delany, who had been my guest for a few weeks, and became, for the time, my fellow traveler. We were paddled up the CAVALLA, a fine, broad-flowing river, running through a rich and populous country, with banks rising twenty, thirty, fifty feet, almost perpendicularly from the water's level, its turning points opening ever and anon to our view grand mountain scenery in the distance, with visions of ravishing beauty now and then bursting upon our sight, navigable for sloops and schooners near eighty miles from the coast, and stretching out beyond the falls which here obstruct its passage, some three or four hundred miles in the interior. Everywhere, in every town, we were most cordially received, hospitably entertained, and my teachings eagerly listened to, by whole towns and villages, who invariably turned out, in a body to hear the preacher. In most of these towns I had gone preaching before; other missionaries had been there long and often before me; and hence you can see that it was interest that excited them, and not mere novelty.

Now here is a vast, open field, ready for the Gospel; but it is but *one* among scores, in the limited territory of Liberia. Saving that the Cavalla can be navigated a further distance inland, there are many other as good opportunities and facilities for the conveyance of the Gospel interiorward, as this.

Now, let me ask, what hinders the colored Christians of America from entering these large, inviting missionary fields, and founding the institutions of christianity here? Putting aside, altogether, the question of colonization, why can they not as a people, come forward to save their race from heathenism, and to give them both the present and the future consolations of religion?

Let me refer in particular, to the three classes of religionists among our brethren, with whom I am more especially acquainted: the Methodists, Presbyterians, and Episcopalians.

The colored Episcopalians are a "small folk," I know, but both of us being churchmen, will make my mention of them excusatory. With three or four of these congregations I am intimately acquainted, and I see no difficulty whatever in the way of their adopting some such plan as this: 1. Preparing, as a commencement, some two or three young men for the ministry, for the special purpose of becoming missionaries to Africa. This, of course, presupposes a regular, systematic effort on the part of the ministers of these churches to interest their people in Africa, and to train them in the *habit* of giving to missions. In this way one young heart and another would ever and anon come forward, anxious to devote itself to the evangelization of Africa. The young men might take theological lessons of the minister, and when prepared, might be placed under the Episcopal authority on this coast, and receive orders. 2. When about sending off the young men, if any pious mechanics, or farmers, or school-masters, desired to devote themselves to the work, the congregation might extend their interest to them as well as to the candidates for orders, and assure them of continued regard and future zeal and self-sacrifice in their behalf.* 3. A company thus formed, might be placed at the disposal of the mission, with the request, perhaps, that they might be located together, as one party; and the church from whence they came, or some two or three colored churches, might regard *that* station as their own,—supply it with school books, farming utensils, clothes for missionaries and converts, and provisions to a greater or less extent; might recruit ever and anon with new schoolmasters, or replace decayed or deceased missionaries,—or take charge of their children, [in America,] and prepare them for the work of their parents, in the future.

This is only an outline of what the few colored Episcopal churches in the United States could do.† Perhaps you say, "this is a large scheme!" I reply without hesitation, that from my knowledge of the wealth that has been concentered in it, St. Thomas' Church, Philadelphia, could have done all this thirty years ago. The expense of a small mission, thus constituted, would not near equal the lavish expenditure of some city congregation of colored people, in balls, parties, fashionable rivalry, jewelry, pic-nics, and the department which is politely termed *cuisine*.

Without entering into details, I merely remark that from their numbers, and the increasing intelligence and learning of their ministers, the Presbyterians could do a larger work than the Episcopalians. They have so many *white* colleges and seminaries opened to them, so many obstacles have been removed out of the way of their aspiring young men, and so wide and warm and hearty is the desire of all classes of white

---

* I regret that the theme before me forbids that I should speak of the almost absolute necessity, in any such scheme, of connecting *manual labor* with missionary effort. Indeed no man should become a *colonist* to Africa whose example is likely to encourage the heathen in their irregular, unsystematic, unplodding modes of labor.

† There are no less than *three* different fields into which effective laborers would likely be welcomed :—the church in Sierra Leone, in Liberia, and in the projected field in South Africa, where the "Cambridge and Oxford" mission intend to establish a colony.

Presbyterians to build up their denomination among the free colored people, that the colored Presbyterian churches could contemplate grand saving schemes for Africa, and undertake at once a large and noble work.

But the "African Methodist Episcopal Church" of the United States has the machinery for a most comprehensive missionary service in Africa. They have a well-tried system; they have experience; they have a large body of ministers; and they have a corresponding body, already in existence, under complete organization, in Liberia,—I mean the "Liberian Episcopal Church." If my old friend, Bishop Daniel A. Payne, would only enter into this work with all that warmth of heart, that energy of purpose, and that burning Christian eloquence, which characterize him, what blessedness would he not impart to this land; what spiritual life would he not diffuse among all the churches of his charge, in America! His people could start a saving, systematized plan, by which health, power, life and energy would be constantly poured, like a living stream, into the corresponding body in this country, and so be diffused throughout the land, to the villages, the hamlets, and the huts of tens of thousands of our needy heathen kin!

I am not blind to difficulties. I know some of the trials of emigration. I have been called to some of the difficulties, not to say severities of missionary life. And therefore I shall be free, I trust, from the charge of flippancy. So likewise I am aware of the peculiar obstacles in the way of our brethren in the States. I, too, am an American black man. I have an acquaintance with obstructive idiosyncracies in them. If you think of hindrances and difficulties specially theirs, I know all about them.

But I say it deliberatively, that the difficulties in the way of our brethren doing a goodly work for Africa, are more subjective than objective. *One of these hindrances is a want of missionary zeal.* This is a marked characteristic of *American* black Christians. I say *American,* for from all I hear it does not characterize our West Indian brethren, and the infant church of Sierra Leone is already, in sixty years from its birth a mother of missions. *This* is our radical defect. Our religion is not diffusive, but rather introversive. It does not flow out, but rather inward. As a people we like religion, we like religious services. Our people like to go to church, to prayer meetings, to revivals. But we go to get enjoyment. We like to be made happy by sermons, singing, and pious talk. All this is indeed correct so far as it goes; but it is only *one* side of religion. It shows only that phase of piety which may be termed the "*piety of self-satisfaction*." But if we are true disciples, we should not only seek a comforting piety, but we should also exhibit an effective and expansive one. We should let our godliness exhale like the odor of flowers. We should live for the good of our kind and strive for the salvation of the world.

Another of these hindrances is what the phrenologists term "*inhabitativeness*,"—the stolid inhabitativeness of our race. As a people, we cling with an almost deadly fixity to locality. I see this on both sides of the Atlantic. Messrs. Douglass and Watkins assail Messrs. Horace Greeley and Gerrit Smith for pointing out this peculiarity of character in our people. But without doubt they tell the truth of us. We are not " given to change." The death of a master, the break up of a family, may cast a few black men from the farm to the city, but they go no further. We lack speculation. Man has been called a creature,

"Looking before and after "——

But not so we. We look where we stand, and but few beyond.

So here, on this side of the water. The colonization-ship brings a few hundred freed men to this west coast of Africa. They gather together in the city of Monrovia, or the town of Greenville, and there they sit, yea, and would sit forever, if it were not for some strong *external* influence which now and then scatters a few, and a precious few, here and there along the coast.

Here then you see, in this same people, on both sides of the waters, an exaggeration of the " home feeling," which is so exceedingly opposite to Anglo-Saxon influences that I wonder that we, who have been trained for centuries under them, have not ere this outgrown it. Sixteen years from the settlement of Plymouth, sixty families started from Boston and cut their way to Windsor, on the Connecticut.* We, in Liberia, have never yet had a *spontaneous* movement of old settlers in a body and with a purpose to a new location. The colored people of Rochester, N. Y., in 1853, I hear, were mostly fugitive slaves. The " Fugitive Slave Law " prompted them to emigrate to Canada ; but proximity determined their choice of a home rather than any large principle. We read in the Acts of the Apostles, that when those who at Stephen's death were persecuted, were scattered abroad, " they went everywhere preaching the word." So when our brethren felt constrained to leave the United States, it was meet, it seems to me, that *some* of them should have thought of Africa and her needs. On the other hand, if Liberians had been duly awake to the welfare of our race, we should have shown our brotherly feeling by inviting the wanderers to our shores.

These *two* hindrances, that is, a lack of missionary zeal and a tenacious hold on locality, will doubtless prevent active efforts for the regeneration of Africa. So, too, they will serve to check commercial enterprise. But as a people, we shall have to rise above these things. The colored churches of America will find, bye and bye, they can retain no spiritual vitality unless they rise above the range of selfish observation to broad, general, humane ideas and endeavors. Self-preservation, self-sustenation, are only single items in the large and comprehensive category of human duties and obligations.

> " Unless above himself, he can erect himself,
> How poor a thing is man."

And this is equally true with regard to Liberian black Christians. Do not think that I pretend to say that we in Africa stand on such a high vantage ground that we can point invidiously at our brethren in America. I have no hesitation in

---

* Bancroft's History of America, ch. ix.

saying, as my own opinion, that in both the respects referred to above, we are more blameworthy than you.

A *third* hindrance may be mentioned here. There will be a reluctance on the part of even some good and zealous Christians to engage in the propagation of the gospel in Africa on the ground " that its ultimate tendency must be to subserve the objectionable scheme of African colonization." But surely any one can see that such an objection is wicked. The gospel *must* be preached in all the world. The master commands it. The history of the church shows that it does not necessarily, if generally, carry colonization with it. But even if in'this particular case, it does so, no Christian has a right to shrink from his duty. And that man must be demented who can not see God's beneficent providence in colonization,—that man blind who does not recognize good and mercy in its work —civil and religious, on the coast of Africa! The duties of our present state are not to be determined by imaginary results or prospective issues. They always grow out of the positive commands of the Bible, or manifest human relations, and *both* fasten the duty upon us to care for the heathen in general, and for our heathen kin in particular.

I have no doubt, however, that every effort that is henceforth made to spread the gospel in Africa, will bring many from the impulse of emigration, to Africa. Up to a certain future, but I hope not distant point in American sentiment, there will be, I feel quite certain, a large exodus of the better, more cultivated, and hence more sensitive minds, partly to Africa, Hayti, Brazil, and the British colonies. Those who " having done all," still STAND, must bear with those who leave. Hayti *needs a* PROTESTANT, Anglo-African element of the stamp Mr. Holly will give her. Jamaica is blessed by the advent in her midst of such a strong-minded, open-eyed, energetic spirit, as my old school-mate and friend, SAMUEL R. WARD. And Liberia's wants in this respect are stronger than either of the above. You should learn willingly to give, even of your best, to save and regenerate and build up the RACE in distant quarters.*

---

* The 2d article of the Constitution of African Civilization Society sets forth my views in better language than my own : The Evangelization and Civilization of Africa and the descendants of African ancestors, *wherever dispersed.*"

You should study to rise above the niggard spirit which grudgingly and pettishly yields its grasp upon a fellow laborer. You should claim with regard to this continent that " THIS IS OUR AFRICA," in all her gifts, and in her budding grace and glory. And you should remember too, with regard to emigrants, the words of that great man, " EDMUND BURKE." " The poorest being that crawls on earth, contending to save itself from injustice and oppression, is an object respectable in the eyes of God and man."

But it is time that I should draw to a close, for I have fallen into a too common fault,—I have made too long a " palaver." My letter has run out to a greater length than I intended. And now I shall weary you no longer.

For near three centuries the negro race in exile and servitude has been groveling in lowly places, in deep degradation. Circumstance and position alike have divorced us from the pursuits which give nobleness and grandeur to life. In our time of trial we have shown, it is true, a matchless patience, and a quenchless hope ; the one prophetic of victory, and the other the germ of a high Christian character, now developing. These better qualities, however, have been disproportioned, and the life of the race in general has been alien from ennobling and aspiring effort.

But the days of passivity should now come to an end. The active, creative, and saving powers of the race should begin to show themselves. The power of the negro, if he has such power, to tell upon human interests, and to help shape human destinies, should at an early day make full demonstration of itself. We owe it to ourselves, to our race, and to our generous defenders and benefactors, both in Europe and America, to show that we are capable " of receiving the seed of present history into a kindly yet a vigorous soil, and [that we can] reproduce it, the same, and yet new, for a future period "*
in all the homes of this traduced, yet vital and progressive race.

Surely the work herein suggested is fitted to just such ends,

---

* Dr. Arnold. Inaugural Lecture.

and is fully worthy the noblest faculties and the highest ambition. If I were aiming but to startle the fancy, to kindle the imagination, and thereby to incite to brave and gallant deeds, I know no theme equal to this in interest and commanding influence. And just this *is* the influence it is now exerting upon passionate and romantic minds, in England and the United States, in France and Germany, in Austria and Sardinia. These civilized States are sending out their adventurous travelers to question, on the spot, the mysterious spell which seems to shut out Africa from the world and its civilization. These enterprising spirits are entering every possible avenue to the heart of Africa, anxious to assure the inner tribes of the continent that the enlightened populations of Europe would fain salute them as brethren, and share with them the culture and enlightenment which, during the ages, have raised *them* from rudeness and degradation, if they can only induce them to throw aside the exclusiveness of paganism and the repulsiveness of barbarism.

But the enlightened sons of Africa in distant lands, are called to a far higher work than even this; a work which as much transcends mere civilization as the abiding interests of eternity outvie the transient concerns of time. To wrest a continent from ruin; to bless and animate millions of torpid and benighted souls; to destroy the power of the devil in his strongholds, and to usher therein light, knowledge, blessedness, inspiring hope, holy faith, and abiding glory, is, without doubt, a work which not only commands the powers of the noblest men, but is worthy the presence and the zeal of angels. It is just this work which now claims and calls for the interest and the activity of the sons of Africa. Its plainest statement and its simplest aspect, are sufficient, it seems to me, to move these men in every quarter of the world to profound sensibility, to deep resolve, to burning ardor. Such a grand and awful necessity, covering a vast continent, touching the best hopes, and the endless destiny of millions of men, ought, I think, to stir the souls of many a self-sacrificing spirit, and quicken him to lofty purposes and noble deeds. And when one considers that never before in human history has such a grand and noble work been laid out in the Divine Providence, before the negro race, and that it rises up before them in its full magnitude now, at the very time when they are best fitted for its needs and requirements, it seems difficult to doubt that many a generous and godly soul will hasten to find his proper place in this great work of God and man, whether it be by the personal and painful endeavors of a laborer in the field of duty, or by the generous benefactions and the cheering incitements which serve to sustain and stimulate distant and tried workers in their toils and trials. "A benefaction of this kind seems to enlarge the very being of a man, extending it to distant places and to future times, inasmuch as unseen countries and after ages may feel the effects of his bounty, while he himself reaps the reward in the blessed society of all those who "having turned many to righteousness, shine as the stars forever and ever."*

---

* Bp. Berkley : "Proposal for supplying churches."

www.ingramcontent.com/pod-product-compliance
Lightning Source LLC
Chambersburg PA
CBHW031805090426
42739CB00008B/1165